# Prosperity
# of the Union

## The Intergovernmental
## Conference of the
## European Union
# 1996

Federal Trust Papers Number Seven

# THE FEDERAL TRUST

The Federal Trust was founded in 1945 to study the future of democratic unity between states and peoples. The principal focus of its work has been the European Union and the United Kingdom's role within it.

The Federal Trust conducts enquiries, promotes seminars and conferences and publishes on a wide range of contemporary issues — most recently (apart from the IGC) on pensions reform and on the European information society. Its current work programme includes a study of public-private partnerships in the European Union.

The Trust has also established a major European education programme for sixth forms, universities and young leaders. It is involved in several projects to enhance the European dimension in the curriculum.

The Federal Trust is the UK member of TEPSA (the Trans-European Policy Studies Association).

PUBLISHED BY THE FEDERAL TRUST
11 TUFTON STREET
LONDON SW1P 3QB

© FEDERAL TRUST FOR EDUCATION AND RESEARCH,
AUGUST 1996

ISBN 0 90157355 8
ISSN 1357 3314

# Federal Trust Round Table

The European Union's Intergovernmental Conference opened in Turin on 29 March 1996. A Federal Trust Round Table was established to discuss in depth the issues raised by the IGC, to monitor the processes of its preparation, negotiation and ratification, and, later, to assess its outcome. A conference was held in London on 11 June, entitled *Dividing the Union? Britain and the IGC*, in which several members of the Round Table participated as well as Michel Petite, head of the Commission's Task Force on the IGC, Lord Howe of Aberavon QC and Hugo Young of *The Guardian*.

The Round Table (and the conference) was chaired by Lord Jenkins of Hillhead, President of the European Commission 1977-81; the rapporteur was John Pinder, Chairman of the Federal Trust; the secretary was Andrew Duff, Director of the Trust, to whom any written comments should be addressed.

The members of the Round Table, shown on the following page, served in an independent capacity and did not represent their organisations. They do not necessarily concur with all the opinions expressed in this **Federal Trust Paper**, but they support its general thrust and welcome it as a contribution to the debate about the future of the Union. The Federal Trust is an independent charity and, as such, holds no political view of its own.

*Prosperity of the Union* is the last in the current series of **Federal Trust Papers**. The others have been:

| No. 1 | *State of the Union* | February 1995 |
|---|---|---|
| No. 2 | *Towards the Single Currency* | May 1995 |
| No. 3 | *Building the Union: reform of the institutions* | |
| | | June 1995 |
| No. 4 | *Security of the Union* | October 1995 |
| No. 5 | *Enlarging the Union* | February 1996 |
| No. 6 | *Justice and Fair Play* | April 1996. |

# Members of the Federal Trust Round Table

# Prosperity of the Union

'The European Council considers that job creation is the principal social, economic and political objective of the European Union and its Member States, and declares its firm resolve to continue to make every effort to reduce unemployment'.

EUROPEAN COUNCIL, MADRID, *15-16 December 1995*

No matter how worthy is the process of European integration, the European Union will command popular support only if it provides good government, especially of economic affairs. The 1996 Intergovernmental Conference (IGC) does not have economic policy at the forefront of its agenda, being mainly concerned with the effectiveness of the common institutions of the Union. Nevertheless, the IGC cannot consider institutions without reference to policy instruments whose purpose is to deliver sustainable economic development. Nor can economic policies be formed successfully without effective institutions. Moreover, the IGC will be much affected by the success of the member states in fulfilling the Union's current central policy objective of Economic and Monetary Union (EMU). Steady progress is being made in adapting the monetary institutions of the Union and in agreeing preliminary macro-economic strategy. The IGC could give a welcome stimulus to these preparations by helping to clarify the political nature of the relationship between the 'ins', the 'pre-ins' and the 'outs' — in other words, those who can and do go forward towards the single currency, those who would but have to wait their turn, and those who won't.

Both the IGC in 1996-97 and EMU in 1999 flow directly from the Treaty of Maastricht, the ratification of which was hampered by a public opinion that had turned hostile towards European integration and to the governments that pursued it in large part because of the sudden and severe economic recession. The ratification of the freshly revised Treaty will be no easier because of the Maastricht experience; on the contrary: populist forces are now ranged against the continuation of European unification in a way they never were before. This time, there are likely to be more referendums in more member states. The prevalence of the economic 'feel-good-factor' may be decisive.

Some of these matters we addressed in our second Federal Trust Paper, *Towards the Single Currency*, which was published in May 1995. [1] We make no apology for returning to them here, a year and a bit later. For economic circumstances have changed: the recession may be over, but the anticipated full recovery is not yet assured; transition to Stage Three of EMU for a majority of member states, leading to the single currency, will not take place at the first opportunity (1997) and may have to go ahead without a majority at the second opportunity in 1999. Europe's competitiveness with the rest of the industrialised world still lacks bite; and, above all, unemployment is still much too high by any economic, social or moral standard.

Unemployment stands at about 11% across the Union, with 7 - 8% a stubborn, structural unemployment. It is highest in Spain, where over 22% are recorded as out of work. There are many causes of such a high level of unemployment, most of them the direct consequence of years of economic mismanagement by member state governments. Rightly or wrongly, however, the European Union is held to share much of the blame — and, in fairness, could do more than it does to address the problem. This has led to a recent, widespread recognition of the importance of the EU being seen to combat unemployment. In December 1995, at their meeting in Madrid, the leaders declared that job creation was their 'principal social, economic and political objective'. [2] In this Paper we look at the validity of that claim, and examine ways in which the European Union really can contribute to the prosperity of its citizens.

## Europe's competitiveness

That Europe finds it difficult to compete in world markets is a surprise to nobody. Over the last twenty years, our competitive position relative to Japan and the USA has shrunk in terms of share of exports in sectors such as information technology, investment in R&D and development of innovatory products. The emergence of the 'Asian tigers', led by Hong Kong, Singapore, Taiwan and South Korea, has further weakened Europe's competitive edge. While the European internal market has led over the years to a dramatic increase in intra-Union trade, trade with the rest of the world has not risen so fast. But the situation is far from ruinous. Compared to most of its industrialised competitors, Western Europe has great assets in terms of social and political stability, education and financial capital. The European Union is still completing the process of turning itself into a big new single market; and new, potentially large, markets in Central and Eastern Europe are opening up. **What is needed if commerce and industry in the EU are to exploit their assets and opportunities is more vigorous modernisation of the structure of the European economy, the continual up-grading of the skills of the workforce, and sustained measures to prevent labour costs from out-pacing productivity.**

These three issues were addressed comprehensively by the White Paper of the Delors Commission, published at the end of 1993, entitled *Growth, Competitiveness, Employment.* [3] A package of bold measures was proposed to induce the birth of the information society, to build a trans-European infrastructure and to develop knowledge and know-how; and a less bold attempt was made to increase the flexibility of the labour market. These actions together, it was argued, would allow the EU fully to exploit the newly-created single market and the long hoped-for monetary stability guaranteed by EMU. The White Paper was accepted by the member state governments and worked on, notably at the Essen European Council in December 1994. Yet practical progress has been slight — especially in building the Trans-

European Networks (TENs) on which so much else depends, but where financial and operational difficulties have fuelled a general air of pessimism.

**One of the most important contributions the IGC could make is to turn around the mood of 'Euro-sclerosis' that seems to have affected much of the leadership of the EU.** An attack on fatalism about economic policy is long overdue. Some scholars have tried: notably, James Meade who argued that full employment and low inflation could be achieved by radical redistributive measures and effective wage restraint. [4] Labour markets may be imperfect, but policies and institutions can still make a difference to the level of employment. [5] The IGC and the next round of European Councils before enlargement is the next, best chance to reinforce the political message that member state governments and the EU institutions must follow policies which are designed to make the Union a permanent and profitable home for capital, skills and technological progress.

**To rid the EU economy of burdens which most of its key competitors do not share it is important to consolidate the administration of the single market, to adapt more quickly to technological change, to reduce the cost of borrowing and to guarantee financial discipline in the public sector.** Concrete steps yet need to be taken to ensure the real completion of the single market itself. The single market programme requires the passage and implementation of EC legislation to accomplish the following:

- to reinforce competitive tendering for public procurement;
- to free up the energy markets of Europe, particularly in electricity supply;
- to liberalise fully and on time the whole telecommunications sector;
- to establish a framework for biotechnology;
- to allow the insurances and pensions industries to work freely in any member state;
- to build the regulatory framework to facilitate private investment in public utilities, especially in transport;

4

- to promote the establishment of European companies.

It is equally vital to prepare to preserve the integrity of the single market under the pressures of 'variable geometry'; if the IGC fails to reunite the fifteen member states there will be a complicated system of differentiated integration where some move forward faster and further than others, perhaps with little more than the core single market still shared in common.

The reinforced integration of the European capital markets, which the accomplishment of all the above implies, has enormous potential both for the increased mobility of labour and for increased levels of financial investment. It has been estimated that EU pension funds could grow nine times to $12.7 trillion by the year 2020 if all national restrictions on the way assets were invested were removed. [6] All of these reforms, while being generally beneficial to the prosperity of the whole of the Union, are closely aligned to a specific British interest because the UK is well advanced along the route of liberalisation and privatisation, and has competitive energy and information technology industries as well as leading-edge legal and financial services.

In completing and upholding the single market, the European Commission does not lack an agenda of work that will contribute directly to the prosperity of the Union. The Commission needs and deserves the firmer backing of member state governments and of both sides of industry — the social partners.

**The European social model**

Clearly, good relations between government and industry are essential to manage such rapid structural change, and the relationship must span the whole European dimension and embrace both sides of industry. The 'social dialogue' between employers and employees is an important part of this process and, although neglected in recent years within the UK, is recognised as such elsewhere. At the heart of the controversy about how to treat the social partners is a serious and fundamental disagreement between the member states about what to do with

Europe's labour market — whether, on the one hand, to deregulate and liberalise so as to achieve maximum flexibility of employment or, on the other hand, to protect existing jobs by sustaining the public sector and restraining competition.

The current trend, more pulled by industry than pushed by governments, is to make the 'European social model' adapt to global realities and to increase labour market flexibility. But the battle is far from over, especially in France and the southern member states, where state industries are still protected against competition, or in Germany, Scandinavia and the Netherlands, where state welfare spending remains burdensome and individual responsibilities light. The laissez-faire British should not underestimate the force on the mainland of the social-Christian perspective that holds to values of solidarity and subsidiarity, and that abhors 'social exclusion'. President Chirac defined the approach recently as follows:

> 'If we are to make a success of globalisation, if we are to shape it rather than endure it, then we shall have to adapt to change without sacrificing our cultural and historical models. That is the reason for our deep commitment to the European social model, founded on social protection in keeping with human dignity, a tradition of social dialogue and negotiation, and the role of the State as guarantor of national cohesion'. [7]

The tension between neo-liberal 'Anglo-Saxon' and neo-corporatist 'Continental' practice is witnessed within all EU institutions. The European Commission is clearly torn between extending its own already extensive powers in the field of competition policy so as to reinforce the drive to liberalisation and, on the other hand, strengthening solidarity by regulation in the social field. Definitively, neither side of the argument can be wholly right: **logic suggests that it must be possible to build a competitive economy with a social conscience.** Such a common-sense approach has been adopted by the Ciampi Group, set up to advise the EU on competitiveness. Ciampi has focused attention especially on the role of Small and Medium-Sized Enterprises (SMEs), and has identified the following necessities:

- the adoption of a European company statute to minimise the cost of doing business in different member states;
- the acceleration of the TENs to provide a fast, efficient infrastructure;
- the enlargement of the Union to expand the size of the single market;
- the encouragement of private enterprise into the financing and running of public utilities;
- market-oriented incentives in order to reach environmental targets;
- re-designing education and training to provide for a life-long 'learning society'. [8]

It is widely acknowledged, even on the political left, that restraining social costs is central to building competitiveness for the long term. That is one reason why EMU, with its disinflationary effects, will be such a historic accomplishment for the Union. Price stability, and wage settlements that do not run ahead of productivity increases, are essential preconditions for consolidating the Union's competitive position relative to the fast emerging economies of Central Europe — and therefore for EU enlargement. In several member states, another prerequisite is the need to reduce state welfare spending on the unemployed. **Fortunately, the Maastricht convergence criteria are being used in all member states, not excluding Britain, to put public finances on a better footing and to force down inflation. The European social model needs to be reformed to fit such novel conditions.** As the White Paper suggested, greater attention should also be paid to raising the value of research, education, training — and re-training. And from industry's point of view, continued deregulation and market liberalisation need to be accelerated, especially in the interests of Small and Medium-Sized Enterprises which now make up over 70% of the private sector workforce. The importance of streamlining Europe's public and financial administration extends to the government of the EU, where officious bureaucracy, slow procedures and arcane regulations would impair competitiveness. **Industry needs a Europe that works**. [9]

Multinational companies based in Europe also need a European Union with a global, rather than a narrowly Euro-centric, perspective. This implies a reappraisal of EC anti-trust policy to permit mergers that reflect global realities. The Commissioner responsible, Karel Van Miert, is quite properly calling for an extension of EU competition powers to take into account emerging markets. However, he is resisting changes in the way the Commission exercises its powers of arbitration in state aids and competition policy. It would be more helpful to companies if the Commission were more open to the possibility of reform.[10]

An additional short-term impediment to Europe's economic performance is the over-valuation of the Deutschmark against the Dollar and the Yen. The scramble to create a single currency forged on the strength of the DM puts undue weight on the nominal exchange rate of the German currency. This means that the earlier the transition to Stage Three can be made the better for all concerned. We return to EMU in the final section.

## The problem with unemployment

Despite the importance of enhancing Europe's competitiveness, much of the official debate in the early stages of the IGC has been about the Union's nearly twenty million unemployed. Jacques Santer, in particular, has seized on employment as the *grand projet mobilisateur* of his Commission Presidency. Not least of the reasons for making employment top priority is that fear of unemployment appears to be undermining confidence in the single currency. Santer proposes to boost spending on key projects by Ecu 1.7 bn before 1999 and to seal an agreement between governments, business and the trades unions to deliver higher productivity and wage restraint. [11] The key projects are those TENs chosen at the Essen European Council from the list advanced in the 1993 White Paper; the proposed expenditure is within the limits of the budgetary ceiling of the Union and is drawn largely from underspending on the CAP and partly from resources originally earmarked for R&D and SMEs; the tripartite *pacte de confiance* is being developed, albeit with some scepticism, through a continuing round of negotiations between the social partners and the Commission at European level.

**One cause of endless frustration is the inability of member state governments to put fine words into practice.** The proposals of the Delors White Paper were designed to revitalise the economy of the Union, and were reinforced by political decision of the highest level at a series of meetings of the European Council. Once left to their own devices, however, the Council of economic and finance ministers (Ecofin) and the Council of labour and social affairs ministers — assisted by an Economic Policy Committee of officials — have tended to prevaricate. In the long term, EMU will establish favourable conditions for investment and growth; since the Essen summit, the EU has a respectable medium-term strategy to combat unemployment; but in the short term the EU institutions find it very difficult to act effectively. Inflexibility in labour markets is a major cause of unemployment. But, apart from the very important matter of free movement across the frontiers between member states, regulation of labour markets is largely a matter for the member states' governments, which often feel themselves subject to electoral constraints. Efforts to encourage the private sector to invest are moreover threatened by nervousness in the capital markets at the Union's overall stability and prospects; while the creation of jobs by direct public financing is prevented by the tough regime of EMU. **While many measures to combat unemployment are possible at the level of the member state and below, it remains the case that the European Union has still to find and establish an effective role for itself.**

Responsibilities of the EU in this regard are far from negligible, and fall into eight fields: general economic policy, competition policy, labour policy, vocational training, regional development, environmental protection, R&D and TENs. The Treaty base for specific action in the field of employment is sound: Article 2 talks, in a bit of a mouthful, of promoting throughout the EU a 'harmonious and balanced development of economic activities, sustainable and non-inflationary growth respecting the environment, a high degree of convergence of economic performance, a high level of employment and of social protection, the raising of the standard of living and quality of life, and economic and social cohesion and solidarity among Member States'. It is clear, however, that the question of employment did not achieve a special emphasis at Maastricht: the Treaty on European Union was negotiated just at the end of a period of sustained growth and rising employment, and the focus was predominantly on ensuring lasting convergence in inflation rates.

To redress the balance, the European Commission has proposed to the 1996 IGC that the Treaty be strengthened in relation to employment, social policy and environmental sustainability. The Commission is backed by the European Parliament and by most member states, and notably by the government of Sweden, where the social consequences of the liberalising forces of European integration are sharply felt. The Commission talks of the need for 'structured and coherent action', and proposes that employment be regarded as a matter of common interest — requiring an additional clause to Article 3 — with the following objectives:

- to establish a common strategy for job creation;
- to stimulate cooperation between the social partners and government;
- to strengthen EU scrutiny of member states' employment policies;
- to ensure that jobs are taken into account in all Community policies. [12]

The European Council at Turin, in March 1996, agreed that the IGC should consider how to reinforce the 'cooperation and coordination' of member states in this area, as well as how to reconcile the rigours of competition with the requirement to ensure universal access to public services. [13] Jacques Santer moved quickly to a final draft of his 'European Pact of Confidence for Employment', in which he proposes to make macroeconomic policy employment oriented, to maximise the contribution of EU policies towards creating jobs and to modernise the labour market. [14] The greatest difficulty in reaching agreement lies in the third area, especially over the definition of working time and the relationship between hours worked on the one hand and social security and vocational training on the other. Santer's goal is to 'launch a collective enterprise involving the public authorities and the social partners alike and defining their respective commitments in a coordinated comprehensive strategy'. [15] The Pact is long and ambitious, with several proposals for new action programmes and task forces. For the IGC the Pact has made good proposals for the strengthening of EU surveillance of national economic policy (Article 103) and for consolidating the Commission's negotiating powers in the World Trade Organisation (Article 113).

At Florence, however, on 21-22 June, the European Council hardly rose to Santer's challenge to 'launch a vast mobilisation for employment'. [16] While the leaders accepted most of the Commission's proposals for further studies, and paid lip service to the need to complete the single market, they refused to increase the expenditure ceiling on the transport TENs. The European Council took note of other proposals, and referred them, and the idea of the Pact itself, to Ecofin.

Whatever the outcome of the IGC debate about inclusion in the Treaty of a new employment clause, no more jobs will be created by the EU unless member state governments will the means as well as stating the objective. **The fact is that employment cannot be tackled directly at EU level unless national sovereignty is pooled in the area of macroeconomic and, to a certain extent, fiscal policy. The public must understand this.** There is a danger that the EU will be blamed for failing to combat unemployment. A clear distinction also needs to be made between short-term and long-term solutions. While EMU and increased competitiveness will help employment in the long run, they might lead initially to job losses. In the field of EU competition policy, on no account must short-term unemployment be used as an excuse to block a competitive merger or to protect the inefficient public sector. [17]

## The importance of Ecofin

In the last resort, the Council of economic and finance ministers is responsible for guiding the macroeconomic policy of the Union and for establishing the fiscal stance of member states. If it is to do its job well, Ecofin needs to reinforce its multilateral surveillance of domestic economic policies, especially for those member states participating in Stage Three of EMU. Under Article 103 of the Treaty of Maastricht, Ecofin must focus on the performance of member states in achieving the EMU convergence criteria. The Council, aided by the Monetary Committee and acting by qualified majority vote (QMV) on a proposal of the Commission, already formulates 'broad guidelines of the economic policies' of the member states and of the Union as a whole. Were a member state to deviate from the guidelines, the Council may issue and publish, again all by QMV, certain recommendations addressed to the government concerned. In grave circumstances the Council can levy penalties to correct 'excessive' deficits.

Ecofin also has the discretionary power, on the basis of a proposal of the European Central Bank (ECB) or the Commission, to determine the external exchange rate of the single currency. Although it may prefer informal arrangements to stabilise the Euro, Ecofin would be wise to adopt a sustainable strategy for the Euro that enhances the global competitiveness of the EU economy.

In addition, Ecofin has the general duty to regard member states' economic policies as 'a matter of common concern', and to coordinate them. [18] This means, in effect, that Ecofin will have to work to resolve any contradictions between the fiscal policies of the member states, while being unable to centralise fiscal policy or to command big resource transfers between the richer and poorer parts of the Union.

The inclusion in the Treaty of what would amount to common employment policy objectives would broaden the scope of the Council's deliberations to incorporate the general economic policy of each government. Doubtless this amounts to a further incursion by the EU on 'national sovereignty', but **it is difficult to see how a single currency regime could work without a supranational body capable of acting like a cabinet charged with executive decision-making over macro-economic policy.** Indeed, many argue, including Jacques Delors, that it would be undesirable to allow the European Central Bank virtually unfettered power to run monetary policy, and that a balance should be struck between technical proficiency and political exigency. **Ecofin has big potential, and on how it now manages to develop its powers depends much of the political case for EMU.** The addition of employment policy, not as a strict convergence criterion affecting the transition to Stage Three of EMU, but as a specific economic objective of the Union, might greatly encourage the mature development of the Council of economic and finance ministers. In turn, its partnership with a strong Ecofin will encourage the ECB to act like the Bundesbank, which is a truly federal bank, with sinews that reach right down to the German provincial banks. **The ECB in Frankfurt, the hub of the European System of Central Banks, will need to work quickly to establish a basis of trust with the central banks of member states comparable to that which pertains in Germany.** Both Ecofin and the ECB also need to develop an effective relationship with the European Parliament and the Commission. The latter is especially responsible under the Treaty for managing the process of consultation with both sides of industry and for building up its own capability to represent the common economic interest of the Union.

## The problem with growth

The overriding concern of Ecofin is likely to be the Union's economic sluggishness, about which there is already palpable anxiety. There is a widespread belief that the Union will never again be able to achieve rates of growth sufficient in themselves to eliminate high unemployment. Until the early 1970s, the West European economy grew at between 3% and 4% per annum. Since then, growth rates have slipped to barely 2%. At this level, and with the increasing productivity of those in work, unemployment can hardly decline. If GDP growth does not comfortably exceed productivity growth, unemployment will remain high. According to the OECD, lacklustre GDP growth has meant that nearly all the EU member states are under-performing. The 'output gap' — the difference between potential and actual GDP — was calculated in 1993 to be 2.7% for Europe as a whole, with only Ireland close to its potential and with Finland as much as 5.7% below.

So the Union faces a serious dilemma. If policy initiatives succeed in promoting more employment at a rate higher than that of GDP growth, productivity will have fallen. Yet rising productivity is seen as essential to bolster Europe's competitiveness. One way out is to reduce the supply of labour by enforcing early retirement or imposing short or part-time working. But political parties that have proposed this, like the French socialists, have been thwarted by the high fiscal cost of such measures.

## Some elements of a programme

The only real answer to the problem of unemployment, therefore, is a high level of growth throughout Western and Central Europe which not only increases the total demand for labour but also creates space for imaginative schemes to spread jobs more widely. So long as the fiscal position of many member states remains precarious, they cannot safely relax their fiscal austerity in order to stimulate a rapid demand for labour. **A substantial revival in employment will require both that low-skilled labour be**

**priced back into employability and that demand expand without fiscal laxity in order to generate a net increase in jobs.** The objective should be several years of growth of demand modestly above the underlying supply-side rate of growth of the economy, stimulated by lower interest rates rather than fiscal expansion.

In certain member states, now that inflation has been overcome, there is some scope for a less austere monetary policy as a means of fostering growth, coupled with innovative supply-side policies. Recent falls in German short-term interest rates to levels last achieved in 1988 are encouraging in this regard. There has also been a shift away from a uniform adherence to financial orthodoxy, as evidenced by the Santer employment initiative. But so far there have been few tangible measures to reduce unemployment, and it falls to the series of European Councils that coincide with the IGC, to stitch together all the elements of a convincing, long-term employment programme. We suggest the following:

> 1. *The White Paper.* The Delors White Paper contained a comprehensive list of proposals for improving the employment situation. The IGC would be wise to do what it can to bring these proposals to fruition. A European Union employment programme would be seen as a determined effort to implement a 'White Paper Plus', in the sense that the single market programme could be seen as the 'common market plus': the 'plus' in that case being principally the instrument of the timetable, the institutional development of qualified majority voting, and strong political commitment on the part of the governments. The 'Plus' for the White Paper, beyond what is already being done to implement it, could include some new projects; a stronger financial base; a timetable for those elements that are amenable to it; a certain extension of qualified majority voting; and a strong political commitment of the governments.

Beyond the governments' commitment, it is now also very important to secure strong support from the civil society and the wider public. Strengthened consultation with the social partners at European level, driven by the aim of reforming the social model, is a particularly significant ingredient of the employment programme. To the present partners — UNICE, representing the employers, ETUC, for the trades unions, and CEEP, for the public enterprises — should be added NGOs and expert groups. The dialogue should be opened up, and made more representative and less confrontational. The role of the Economic and Social Committee in modernising the European social model might be significant.

2. *The Single Market.* The main contribution of the Union towards creating a context that encourages business activity and investment has been the single market programme. **Completion of the programme is, as the White Paper emphasised, essential for the future health of the European economy and hence for employment.** But while the Cecchini report did much to establish the merits of the single market programme in the eyes of business, its credibility for the public has been dimmed by the subsequent recession. It is not easy for citizens to distinguish between conjunctural causes of the level of employment and the longer-term determinants. The state of the economy is now somewhat better, and the public may therefore become more inclined to accept that the single market is fundamentally a job-creator. There is urgent need of a major 'Cecchini 2' study that would seek to distinguish between the respective effects on employment of the recession, of technological change and of the single market programme, and also bring into focus the benefits that can be expected over the longer term.

3. *Labour markets.* Much of the White Paper was about the need for social solidarity in the face of labour market reform. Labour market reforms required in most EU

member states include reducing the duration of special benefit payments for the unemployed, greater flexibility in the minimum wage for young people, restructuring payroll taxes and integrating the tax and social security systems. The Union's role is not so much of legislation and policy-making, but rather of encouraging the member states to act. One helpful method is that of 'peer review', as is practised for macroeconomic policy; and this can be accompanied by a 'scoreboard', in which the actions taken by member states are reported in a regular annual survey. The studies on jobs by the OECD are already helpful in this regard, and the more the results of these surveys are publicised, the more effective they are likely to be.

The Union also has its own part to play, in removing the obstacles to cross-frontier movement of workers and encouraging the skills that make such movement feasible. This is not only of interest to many citizens, but also relevant to the success of EMU in the long run, because disequilibria in the relationship between different regions and states are easier to correct if obstacles to the movement of labour are removed. Mobility of labour implies a search for work across the Union: the need to adapt EU rules on unemployment benefit for persons looking for a job in another member state is pressing. [19]

4. *Life-time education and training.* Here again the field is mainly for the member states. But the Union has a legitimate role particularly in promoting those elements of life-time education and training that are relevant to cross-frontier employment: knowledge of languages, cultures and institutions to enable people to make the most of the Union-wide employment market, as well as to exercise their rights and perform their duties as Union citizens. The Erasmus and Socrates programmes provide good examples for this at the level of higher education, and Leonardo in vocational training. The principle could be extended, much more generously than at present, first for the training of

young people other than those in higher education; and secondly, for people of other age groups. The Commission must sponsor educational opportunities for both young and non-young people to study matters relevant to European citizenship, such as the languages and cultures of the member states, the history and workings of the Union institutions, and EC law.

A European voluntary civilian service, with young people working in multinational groups on European technical, environmental and humanitarian projects, could if developed on a sufficiently large scale contribute significantly to the reduction of youth unemployment. A proposal to this effect has been taken up for the IGC by the institutions and the member states; this is to be welcomed.

5. *Environment Policy*. The relevance of environmental policy to the creation of employment, as explained in the Delors White Paper, is central. Energy conservation is a vast challenge for the Union that has relevance in every member state and at all levels of society. **The proposal for an eco-tax, the revenues from which would make possible the reduction of taxes on employment, in particular for low-paid workers, is a crucial part of the equation.** A rigorous approach to the reduction of pollution from carbon dioxide and general energy is essential if the EU is to meet its international targets. For reasons of competitiveness, any harmonised tax proposal has to be made fiscally neutral, either by reducing VAT or by shifting taxation away from income and labour. The latter approach will help the fight against unemployment in the Union, perhaps by half a million jobs. [20]

Genuine environmental taxes can be feasible only on an EU-wide level, and we return below to the question of whether such a source of revenue should become one of the 'own resources' of the Union itself. It may be difficult to present environmental taxation as a major element in the European Union's popular front, but there is at least widespread public support (66%) in favour of EU decision-making to combat pollution and global-warming. [21] In spite of British opposition, the European Commission should revisit its eco-tax proposals as soon as possible. Several member states, including the Italians who presided over the opening of the IGC, are in favour of extending QMV to the question of eco-taxation. [22]

There is pressure for a thorough 'greening' of the Treaty to make sustainable development a core objective of the Union. [23] The Commission proposes two Treaty changes to the IGC on environmental policy. First, that 'the right to a healthy environment, and the duty to ensure it' should become one of the elements of EU citizenship; and second, that environmental objectives should be specifically incorporated into all the sectoral policies of the Union. [24] It is also important for the IGC to clear up the confusion left by Article 130s of Maastricht between the use of QMV and co-decision in some areas of environmental policy, and, in others, unanimity with the Parliament only consulted. If there was once a rhyme and reason to this differentiation, it has since been forgotten. To accompany reform of institutional procedures, there should be a shift of emphasis from a regulatory approach to the setting of quantitative environmental standards to a market-oriented approach which spreads the costs of environmental measures across European industry as a whole. Taxes, incentive schemes and tradable permits, coupled with a wide degree of discretion about how environmental goals are to be reached, will reinforce Europe's competitiveness. Blanket regulation tends not to be cost-effective; nor does it spur innovation. Basic EU-level environmental and food hygiene standards will however remain necessary, rigorously enforced.

6. *Research and technological development.* This too is the subject of a chapter in the White Paper. Alone, member states are disadvantaged at the cutting edge of science and technology; but together, avoiding duplication and pooling resources, they can compete on equal terms with the USA and Japan. This is obvious to three-quarters of public opinion. [25] Yet member states resisted the budgetary expenditure on R&D recommended by the Commission at the Edinburgh meeting of the European Council in December 1992, and a reduced package was eventually agreed of Ecu 12.3 bn over the period 1994-98. Among the R&D projects that could be especially stimulating for employment over the medium and longer term are those contributing to the development of sectors connected with Information Technology and with the creation of the Europe-wide network of information highways. [26] Among Treaty changes required of the IGC, is the application of QMV and co-decision to the Union's multi-annual framework programme on research and technology (Article 130i). The UK prime minister was proud of his stand against this at Maastricht, but British industry has paid the price for the faltering drive to build the information society in Europe.

7. *Local development.* Much new employment will be generated by local initiatives. The Commission has indicated the potential in a sample of seventeen fields from tree-planting to child care and home-helps. [27] While public policy to encourage and facilitate such initiatives will come mainly from within the member states, the Union can help the development of such policy through cooperation and exchange of information among them and should actively support local initiatives that come within the scope of the Structural Funds or can otherwise be seen to have a European dimension. Careful disbursement of EU funding can stimulate partnerships between the public and private sectors that are geared to meet the needs of Europe's changing social fabric,

especially in inner cities. The Commission estimates that up to 400,000 jobs could be created each year by a sustained and dynamic programme of local development initiatives.

8. *Trans-European Networks*. TENs for the transport of people, goods, energy and information have great potential for the creation of employment over the medium and long term. While IT and telecoms need liberalisation and regulatory reform, transport needs some public finance.

To date, fourteen transport schemes have been chosen, at a total cost of Ecu 91 bn, and ten energy projects, costing Ecu 5 bn; various environmental and telecommunications networks are being studied. Over the medium term, employment is generated through the construction of the infrastructure. (We take issue with those economic studies that deny their employment potential.) In the long term, a first class infrastructure is a necessary condition for dynamic investment in a region of the world such as Europe. [28] The growing proportion of new investment that will be located in those parts of the world which offer the most attractive conditions will be greatly influenced by the quality of the infrastructure (and also of the environment); and in addition to the benefits for employment in the long term, the prospect of a more dynamic European economy in the next century would help to generate investment and growth, and hence employment, in the shorter term too. **TENs should be seen as the physical aspect of the completion of the single market, as well as an instrument for enabling European citizens to participate fully in the society and the polity.** They must be of special significance for the integration of Central and East European as well as of other peripheral regions, including British and Irish, into the Union's mainstream. They should also be attractive for Germany, strengthening the links of Central and Eastern Europe with Western Europe, and providing a boost for economic activity and employment in the eastern Länder in particular, in which key sectors of many such TENs would be located. The information highways and the associated IT will moreover be central to the economic and societal development of the coming decades.

The TENs are already a major Union activity. If they are seen more clearly as an essential element in the development of the European economy and the creation of jobs over the medium and longer term, it should be possible to secure for them a higher priority. This should bring with it a more ample financial base, including both budgetary allocations and joint financing by private and public capital.

9. *Small and Medium-Sized Enterprises.* The completion of legislation to harmonise conditions of establishment for companies across the Union would cut out much of the current bureaucratic nightmare, which is especially debilitating for SMEs. Improving the financial environment by deregulation and, of course, by the introduction of the single currency will give SMEs better access to the integrating European capital market. The Commission should take more seriously its duty to undertake cost-benefit analyses of proposed EU measures. [29] But stronger links also need to be built between the research and technology community, the financiers and the entrepreneurs — and on a trans-European basis — if SMEs are to reach the high levels of growth that Europe needs. Much has been done by the Commission's horizontal action programmes so far: now a more concerted effort is needed to bring the fruits of R&D to commercial exploitation. A European 'technology foresight' programme has been recommended by Ciampi; more seed corn and venture capital funding is also required, with projects appraised by a partnership team of recognised technical and business expertise. The Luxembourg-based European Investment Fund should provide for a higher percentage of loans to innovative SMEs. [30]

10. *Lightening the administration.* Public administration throughout Europe is, on the whole, ponderous and second-rate. The addition of a European Union level of regulation and bureaucracy to existing national, regional and local administration could be crippling to enterprise. This aspect of the recent federalisation process in Belgium is an example to us all (not to be followed). Other advanced industrial countries with which Europe competes are making strenuous efforts to reduce their own regulatory burdens; Europe must do likewise. [31] In previous *Federal Trust Papers* we have written of the need to simplify, codify and rationalise the Union's legislative acts, and to keep them proportionate to the scale of the problem in hand. [32] The same applies to regulation affecting health and safety at the work place, consumer and environmental protection, technical standardisation, commercial rules of origin and public procurement, as well as to many aspects of daily life, such as banking, health care and insurance, that are unnecessarily complicated to conduct — especially for non-nationals. The transposition of EU single market directives into member state law seems to be highly prone to over-elaborate ornamentation by national officials, especially in Britain. As the Economic and Social Committee has observed repeatedly, poor regulation officiously applied impairs the full operation of the single market, thereby reducing trade. [33]

11. *Tax reform.* Rules are nowhere more ornate than rules about tax, and the Union's first, botched attempt to harmonise VAT is a prime example. Moreover, the liberalisation of capital has had unsettling effects upon the tax regimes of the member states, and has increased the potential for tax avoidance and the degradation of fiscal revenues at a time when fiscal prudence, and the Maastricht criteria in particular, make this extremely undesirable. The tendency among member state governments has been to increase the taxation of labour, which is largely immobile. For the sake of boosting employment, this trend must be

rapidly reversed. **Too many low-skilled people are being priced out of jobs by marginal rates of tax (and means-tested benefits): they need to be priced back into jobs by tax reform**, but without depressing wages to anything like the degree that has occurred in the USA. This suggests **the need for the introduction across the EU of modest, regionally determined minimum wages, encouraged and coordinated by the institutions of the Union**.

Approximation of rates of VAT and excise duties has been very slow. Salaries, social security, mortgages, insurance and pensions are very difficult to carry across the internal borders of the Union without serious tax penalties. In fact tax is another and important obstacle to the smooth functioning of the single market. What is required is a simple tax system which treats intra-Union transactions like domestic ones. The Commission also broaches the question of the Council voting procedure on taxation matters. The requirement for unanimity has meant that almost no real progress has been made on tax legislation and a spurious defence of national sovereignty has led to a real loss of fiscal control to market forces. [34]

**The European Union will tread carefully in fiscal matters; but it should be as bold as possible.** While the Union's institutions have few direct powers to intervene in the economic management of a member state, they and the European-level political parties should become a powerful influence on the intellectual and political environment of the member states, especially with regard to the fiscal component of macro-economic policy.

12. *Qualified Majority Voting.* Following the example of the single market programme, the employment programme will be facilitated by extending the provision for qualified majority voting in the fields of regional, industrial and environmental policy. Since the British Conservative government has been the most stubborn opponent of

provision for more majority voting, and a general election is looming, it is relevant that both the Labour Party and the Liberal Democrats favour action at the IGC, as do most of the other member states, to extend QMV in those areas. [35]

The theme of employment is attractive to both citizens and governments, provided that a programme can be credible. It is suggested that enhanced Union action can make a significant difference for both the shorter and the longer term, in the European dimensions of the fields listed above. Citizens might not appreciate this difference in the shorter term if the benefits were outweighed by conjunctural job losses. But the second half of this decade should be a period of economic upswing; and when business people are confident that the single currency will before long be introduced, an investment boom should follow, as it did after the launching of the single market programme. The prospects for reducing unemployment are therefore good: the Union's employment programme should have a fair wind behind it. It should be possible to persuade citizens not only that the Union is not a net destroyer of jobs, but also that it is essentially creative in this as in other ways.

**The Social Protocol**

One of the trickier dossiers on the table of the Intergovernmental Conference is how to treat social policy. Since the declaratory Social Charter was signed in December 1989 (though not by Mrs Thatcher), the Commission has proposed 47 directives and regulations covering health and safety, equal treatment of women, workers consultation, special treatment of part-time workers, the young, the elderly and the disabled, and so on. Some of the proposals enacted in EC law, notably those affecting health, safety and equal treatment, have had a very significant impact. Most member states would like to persist with the approach adopted, and would accept a further raft of social reforms driven by the European Union. This makes the United Kingdom's notorious derogation from the social chapter of the Treaty of Maastricht increasingly contested. The European Commission, backed by fourteen member states and by the European Parliament, insists on the abolition at the IGC of the Social Protocol: 'The social dimension should be one of the central themes of the Conference. Above all there has to be a common base of social rights for all Union citizens.' [36]

The Social Protocol extends the powers of the European Community to new areas and enhances the importance of the social dialogue in the legislative process. The Protocol helps the Commission to consult with the two sides of industry in the preparation of legislation, and greatly enhances the role of the social partners in implementing EC policy. Although QMV is introduced for the passing of measures to improve working conditions, to inform and consult labour, to ensure equality of treatment between men and women, and to combat social exclusion, unanimity is required for matters concerning social security, labour contracts, collective bargaining, employment of third country nationals and EU-level job creation schemes. Questions of pay, the right of association and the right to strike are explicitly excluded. In spite of these caveats, the British prime minister was and remains greatly agitated by the Social Protocol. John Major says:

> 'The Social Chapter should be seen for what it is: a 'European jobs tax'. A tax on jobs by the front door and, in time, a tax on jobs by the back door. That's why it's immoral. That's why, if I'd signed the Social Chapter, I could never have looked the unemployed in the eye again'.[37]

We well understand the reluctance of the British Conservative government to encumber industry with social regulation to improve workers' conditions while taking no account of business cost; we agree very much with its determination to consolidate the single market and to oppose unwelcome protection; and we share its concern that low-skilled labour can be quickly priced out of jobs by minimum standards centralised at EU level. On the other hand, we believe that each social measure should be treated on its own merits and not as an enemy sortie in a great ideological battle; that workers in the newly liberalised single market need a certain level of protection; and that people generally work better if they are treated well.

The Social Protocol has been used only rarely, where the opposition of the UK shuts all other avenues. To date, only two pieces of legislation, the Works Council Directive and the Parental Leave Directive, have been promulgated under the terms of the Social Protocol — with the latter being formulated by the social partners. [38] The existence of the British opt-out has two disadvantages and two perverse consequences. First, the integrity of EC law is damaged by being unevenly applied in different member states; second, the single market is vulnerable to disputes over distortions of competition; third, thirteen large British firms operating both within and without the UK are choosing in any case to apply their labour relations policy uniformly across the Union, ignoring the British opt-out; and fourth, European social policy is now being shaped ineluctably without a British voice at the table.

It is our view, all things considered, that **the UK would be wise to agree to its partners' unanimous request to incorporate the provisions of the Social Protocol into the main Treaty**. If it is true, as the British government often claims, that the debate about the future of the European social model is favouring the 'Anglo-Saxon' approach, the UK has nothing to fear from surrendering its derogation. In any case, it will be better for the UK to be in the position to help shape policy from the inside.

### The EU budget

Relatively small as it is, the EU budget cannot assume a major role in combating unemployment and in building the prosperity of the Union. Nevertheless, EU direct spending has a significant part to play, both actually and symbolically, in the whole scheme of things; and it is certainly relevant to consider whether the EU budget needs reform.

The history of the European Union budget is one of irregular evolution in the sources of revenue. A system of 'own resources' was introduced properly from 1979, drawn from customs duties, agricultural levies, and a levy on the VAT tax base — which now accounts for over half the total revenue. A fourth own resource, based on GNP, was added in 1988, now accounting for about one third of the total. Every so often, multi-annual 'financial perspectives' are agreed to cap the growth of the budget: the current package, whose ceiling will be 1.27% of GDP or approximately Ecu 100 bn, runs out in 1999. The negotiation of its successor, which is certain to be controversial, will take place immediately after the conclusion of the IGC. The new size and shape of the Union budget will have to take into account the likely future enlargement towards Central and Eastern Europe.[39] The three most thorny items in the negotiation are likely to be the reform of the CAP, which accounts for about half of EU spending; the reform of the structural funds, amounting to over a third of the total; and the UK rebate. There is, too, a fourth problem, that of fraud.

The EU budget is an area where QMV has been used for many years by the Council, and the European Parliament is a real partner in settling the annual budget. However, an arcane but significant distinction between obligatory spending (formally arising directly out of the Treaty, and in practice largely agricultural) and non-obligatory spending has been used to restrict the powers of the Parliament mainly to the latter. **A major decision is required of the IGC to abolish this distinction, and thereby to make the Parliament a fully co-equal partner with the Council.**

1. *The future of farming.* Jacques Santer has suggested, as part of his solidarity pact on employment, that any underspending from the CAP should be transferred to stimulate the building of the TENs. Whether there will be any significant underspending on the CAP is largely a matter of the fluctuations in world prices and of the European currencies against the US dollar, and it can easily be swallowed up by unforeseen developments like the cost of eradicating mad cow disease and restoring the confidence of Europe's beef-eaters.

The future of the CAP is not inevitably part of the agenda of the IGC. But it is a significant element of the context, and to ignore the CAP entirely would be to fail to prepare the Union effectively for enlargement, in terms not just of budgetary cost, but also of competitiveness and employment.

Two-thirds of the Union's population now lives in one hundred conurbations; the remaining third occupies the 80% of the territory of the Union which is rural. The drift of labour away from farming and fishing continues, especially among the young. Schools and shops close and public transport and social services wither: the pattern is all too familiar and common throughout Western Europe. Jobs must return to the countryside if rural communities are not to die and, especially in the hillside, farmland not be laid to waste. There is plenty of work to be done in terms of modernisation of agriculture; tourism and recreation; environmental improvement; and the development of renewable energy sources. The extension of 'Network Europe' will also make it easier for professionals to live in and work from the countryside. The impact of the 1992 MacSharry reforms is already being felt, but much more remains to be done to reduce prices towards world market levels and to replace price support with more targeted aid to the rural sector. [40] A reduction of total agricultural spending would moreover free resources for investment in employment creating projects such as the Trans-European Networks.

The question arises for the IGC: is the current Treaty sufficient as a legal base and as a political package deal on which to carry through such radical reform? Article 39 of the Treaty of Rome was written in 1957. **Today the Union has new objectives for the countryside that would include sustainable development, the protection of nature, food hygiene, land use and planning, and diversity of employment opportunities.** A revision to the Treaty along these lines would underscore the changes which need to be made to existing policies. [41]

2. *Reform of the structural funds.* The bulk of the European Union's structural funds comprise, first, the Regional Development Fund whose purpose is to supplement member state spending on economic development in the peripheral or frontier regions; secondly, the Social Fund, whose aim is to increase the quantity and value of vocational training in order to combat social exclusion, especially among women and the young; and thirdly, the Cohesion Fund, which was set up by Maastricht to give practical help to Greece, Ireland, Portugal and Spain in the field of transport networks and environmental improvements (particularly water management). About 80% of the funds are administered by member state governments.

Although one may be cynical about how they are used and misused, the importance of the structural funds to the poorer EU economies cannot be overstated: they comprise 7% of Portugal's GNP, and the Brussels bounty has contributed to Ireland's extraordinary economic success in recent years. [42] Nevertheless, reform is required for what has become a very large item of EU expenditure.

**The Structural Funds need objectives that are clearly specified, effective financial management, and an end to the confusion about who is responsible for what. This means that the executive powers of the Commission need to be reinforced.** The stipulation about involvement of complementary public finance, from national, regional or local authorities, has to be more closely scrutinised: this implies a stronger, more hands-on Commission, as national governments are inevitably compromised in monitoring 'additionality'. The objectives of the funds should be reoriented towards assisting the implementation of the policies outlined above, such as the TENs, and in adding value specifically in the interests of the European Union citizen according to the principle of subsidiarity. The large expertise of the European Investment Bank should be tapped to make the structural funds more sharply focused: in 1995 the EIB, which is now the world's biggest international lender and borrower, lent Ecu 18.6 bn within the EU, mostly to underdeveloped regions. [43]

Such a reform of the structural funds implies that some traditional recipients of EU subsidy would cease to be eligible. Moreover, when the reform is placed, as it must be, firmly within the context of enlargement, it is clear that some poorer areas of the richer member states will cease to benefit automatically from EU grants and that the poorer member states of the current Union will get less. All this reduces the chance of effecting reform of the structural funds in the first place. But at present, the structural funds can only be amended by unanimity. **The IGC is faced with the problem that unless QMV is introduced (to Article 130d) the prospect of structural fund reform must be minimal.**

3. *The British problem.* Because the CAP dominates the budget, and the structure and size of farming is so varied throughout the Union, the budget behaves capriciously. The UK, with its small farm sector and its large farm imports from outside the EU, has been the second largest net contributor to the EU budget despite being poorer in terms of GDP than the EU average. Belgium, Denmark and Luxembourg are among the richest member states, and yet are net recipients. However, for obvious reasons the British rebate is increasingly unacceptable to other member states, especially Germany, Austria and the Netherlands. [44] In balance sheet terms, CAP reform will be of relative benefit to the UK but structural fund reform will not, leaving the net effect on the UK contribution to the EU broadly neutral. One of the priorities of UK policy in the imminent negotiations, therefore, must be either to retain some, possibly modified, element of budgetary rebate or to bring about some other reform of the own resources system to render the rebate unnecessary. Here the debate about a possible new fifth element of revenue to the EU budget begins.

Protocol No. 15 of the Treaty of Maastricht, on economic and social cohesion, declares the intention of the EU to take more account of the relative prosperity of the member states in the own resources system, and to examine means of correcting the regressive elements in the existing system (notably, agricultural levies and VAT). The question of regressivity was already well argued in the MacDougall Report in 1977. [45] What is needed now is a new progressive element to finance the Union budget so that the principle of fair burden-sharing is respected. The bitter debate about the UK is really about progressivity — or the lack of it — and the British government would be wise to champion the cause of progressivity on behalf of all the poorer member states of the Union, actual and potential, rather than try to plead a special case on the grounds of national interest. [46]

A radical solution would be to levy an EU surcharge to member states' income and corporation taxes — either indirectly, adjusted on an income per capita basis from the EU average, or falling directly on individual tax-payers and firms. It would be introduced so as to be fiscally neutral, with compensating reductions in the VAT levy. Such a hypothecated tax would certainly be a striking stimulus to citizen identification with the European Union, and would also imply, in institutional terms, a big increase in the financial autonomy of the Union and an inevitable extension of the budgetary powers of the European Parliament to cover revenue as well as expenditure. There are, however, two problems: such a system would require a standardised basis of taxation between the member states, and, as the Commission's tussle with VAT has shown, this is unlikely to be forthcoming; and, secondly, while progressive, an EU income or corporation tax would not serve the cause of boosting employment.

An alternative approach, suggested earlier, would be to make the eco-tax belong either in whole or in part to the Union. Shifting taxation from social security contributions on to environmental poisoning is a potent possibility for making more jobs. None the less, this would not, at least initially, guarantee the progressivity of the own resources system as some of the poorer industrialised regions of the Union (and Central Europe) are more profligate users of non-renewable energy than more advanced regions in the richer member states. Ultimately, however, **once tough environmental policies had worked their way through to improve industrial competitiveness across the Union, an EU eco-tax would have the desired progressive effect on the budget while also favouring growth and employment.**

# $CO^2$ Emissions Per Capita 1994
### (in tonnes)

| | |
|---|---|
| Luxembourg | 29.9 |
| Denmark | 12.1 |
| Finland | 11.9 |
| Belgium | 11.6 |
| Germany | 11.0 |
| Netherlands | 10.7 |
| UK | 9.4 |
| Ireland | 8.9 |
| *EU 15* | *8.3* |
| Greece | 7.5 |
| Austria | 7.0 |
| Italy | 6.9 |
| Sweden | 6.4 |
| France | 6.0 |
| Spain | 5.8 |
| Portugal | 4.6 |

Sources: *Eurostat* News Release No. 25/96 and *Agence Europe*, 29 April 1996.

The choices about budgetary reform are not easy, but they will not be facilitated by refusing to address all the options. The present system is shot full of anomalies, and no amount of tinkering with it will produce the planned, redistributive budget that the EU requires. [47] This IGC, and the parallel negotiations on the new financial perspective, are the place and the time to make a fresh start.

4. *Fraud.* Any reform of the EU budget must have as a high priority the battle against embezzlement. In recent years, the Commission has made big strides in tightening up its financial control yet the Court of Auditors complains habitually about lax procedures concerning how EU funds are spent. (Its recent estimate was that 14% of EU spending suffered from poor monitoring; in 1995 the Commission investigated 4750 cases of malpractice involving Ecu 1.15 bn or 1.4% of the budget.) The

incidence of criminal fraud as against plain incompetence is much over-represented by an inherently hostile media, especially in the UK, but there is a serious danger in the context of EU enlargement that fraud will increase exponentially.

The potential for fraud would be much reduced if the quality of the drafting of EU legislation were improved, as we have suggested elsewhere, and if the Commission had proper resources and competences. [48] At the moment, it is left largely to member state governments to combat fraud both within their own administration and within that of regional and local government. There is a strong case for giving the Commission the same powers of scrutiny over transnational fraud as it has to investigate breaches of EU competition law. Moreover, the system of penalties that the Commission can already impose on member state governments for misuse of CAP spending should be extended to cover the structural funds. Commissioner Liikanen puts proper emphasis on improved financial management, and this means that the Commission must be more obviously in charge of the EC budget as well as more coherent internally. It is also vital that the accountancy profession play a dynamic role in integrating its very diverse practices across the Union. [49]

**EMU: towards Stage Three**

The single currency is designed to be the keystone in a stable and solid structure for the European economy which will provide a framework for its dynamism in the future. The removal of currency risk and the completion of this element of the single market will encourage investment for the longer term, to the lasting benefit of competitiveness and employment. [50] Since the publication of *Towards the Single Currency*, however, the debate about Economic and Monetary Union has risen in temperature and thickened in density. In the United Kingdom the debate has become excessively partisan. For the present British government the peremptory ejection of sterling from the Exchange Rate Mechanism in September 1992 remains a dark hour. Ministers are refusing to budge from the official position that a decision about UK transition to Stage Three of EMU will be taken if and when circumstances permit. The evolution of the politics of the Conservative Party, however, have reduced the chances that a Conservative government will be able to take the plunge whatever the circumstances. Labour says unhelpfully that the issue of the single currency 'must be determined by a hard-headed look at its economic practicalities', though its 1995 policy statement gave a more positive impression. [51]

On the mainland, too, even in Germany, opinion has wavered. Conflicting analyses abound, even from those bankers and ministers most crucially involved at the time, about the merits of what was agreed at Maastricht. No wonder the public seems perplexed. It is difficult not to sympathise with Valéry Giscard d'Estaing, one of the authors of the Exchange Rate Mechanism, who complained in February 1996:

> 'Later, when one speaks of the fourteen different currencies used in the Union, it will seem like a joke. When one explains that this was the system described as ideal, that must be protected and preserved, all this will seem quite extraordinary'.

One of the most robust defences of EMU is heard from the current Irish president of Ecofin, Ruairi Quinn, who argues that his country's drive towards stable exchange rates, lower interest rates, improved access to continental markets and stronger flows of direct investment have set the framework for a successful 'Programme for Competitiveness and Work'. [52] Ireland's experience suggests that the mixture of EU macro-economic policy and domestic employment innovation produces the elusive virtuous circle of strong growth and job creation — even if unemployment in Ireland still stands at over 14%.

Small countries, such as Ireland, have been quicker to understand the importance of creating rules to govern fiscal matters in the single currency regime. The British have been characteristically averse to the German proposal for a sub-treaty Stability Pact among those member states proceeding to the single currency. But such a concept had always been envisaged by the authors of the Treaty, who left the whole question of what kind of monetary policy the Union would adopt, including the matter of inflation targets and exchange rate policy, to the institutions. One option is to add employment criteria to the terms of the Stability Pact: this would have the merit of avoiding the need for Treaty change. It would also be consistent with Ecofin's function, noted above, of reaching a collective position on a fiscal policy that is both compatible with monetary policy and appropriate for Europe's macroeconomic strategy.

A separate set of issues concerns the relationship between those who make the transition to the single currency and those who do not. Here progress has also been difficult, with the UK resisting the idea that a new or thoroughly revised ERM is needed after Stage Three to associate the Euro with those currencies that do not make the transition.

At the informal meeting of Ecofin in Verona in April 1996, British objections were overruled and outline agreement was reached on setting up a new ERM. Under the proposed new arrangement, membership will not be compulsory — which factor sets up another imminent hazardous decision for the UK. It is likely to be up to the ECB and not a member state government to trigger currency realignment. Although the Bank will have only a limited obligation to intervene to support the currencies of those outside the core, it will have strong powers of surveillance. Another important difference between the old and new style ERM is that it will anchor exchange rates in broad bands around the Euro rather than, as at present, around each other. An ERM on these lines is likely to be more stable. [53]

**Will it happen?**

Disappointing rates of growth, lower than anticipated tax revenue and stubborn public deficits have raised doubts about the ability of the EU to effect the transition to Stage Three of EMU by the appointed date of 1 January 1999. The possibility of an orderly delay is inscribed in the Treaty. Under the terms of Article 109j.4, any decision to delay Stage Three must be taken before the end of 1997. The Commission and the EMI were to report on progress made towards meeting the statutory requirements and towards fulfilling the convergence criteria to the Dublin European Council in December 1996. [54] But this requirement, which would have set up the first (and best) occasion to decide on a delay to the timetable, was deemed not to be necessary by the Florence European Council in June 1996 — a curious decision whose affect is unclear.

It should be noted, moreover, that, at the behest of the Commission and the European Monetary Institute, all member state governments, not excluding that of the UK, have repeatedly confirmed their intention to stick rigidly to all the original deadlines, procedures and criteria. [55] Commissioner de Silguy remains optimistic. [56] The Madrid European Council in December 1995 confirmed that the political will exists among the UK's partners to make EMU work and to make it do so according to the schedule and the criteria of the Maastricht Treaty. Accordingly, at their Verona meeting, the ministers set the date of 2002 as a possible second target for those that will miss out on 1999. In the Table below we set out our present assessment of where member states will be in 1997. [57]

In reaching the historic decision about the transition to Stage Three, due in the spring of 1998, the political commitment on the part of France and Germany, in particular, will ensure that Stage Three goes ahead with at least an essential core of member states, provided that they satisfy a reasonable interpretation of the criteria. France and Germany may fail to reduce their public deficits to the 'reference value' of 3% in 1997; but the notion that the Treaty sets a rigid limit of 3% is a fallacy peddled equally by Eurosceptics and fiscal conservatives. What the Treaty requires is that the ratio 'has declined substantially and continuously and reached a level that comes close to the reference value', or is 'exceptional and temporary' and 'remains close to the reference value'. The decision can also take into account the

## The EMU Convergence Criteria in 1997 [59]

*Per cent*

| | Consumer price inflation | Government long-term interest rate | General government deficit/GDP | Gross government debt/GDP | Stable exchange rate 1996-97 |
|---|---|---|---|---|---|
| Austria | 1.6 | 6.6 | 3.1 | 74 | yes |
| Belgium | 1.8 | 6.8 | 3.7 | 131 | yes |
| Denmark | 2.4 | 7.5 | 0.6 | 69 | yes |
| Finland | 1.5 | 7.3 | 1.6 | 63 | yes |
| France | 1.6 | 6.8 | 3.0 | 58 | yes |
| Germany | 1.6 | 6.3 | 2.9 | 62 | yes |
| Greece | 7.0 | n/a | 6.9 | 111 | no |
| Ireland | 2.4 | 7.7 | 1.6 | 77 | yes |
| Italy | 3.5 | 10.4 | 5.2 | 123 | no |
| Luxembourg | 2.1 | 6.5 | - 0.3 | 7 | yes |
| Netherlands | 2.0 | 6.3 | 2.9 | 79 | yes |
| Portugal | 3.0 | n/a | 3.7 | 72 | ? |
| Spain | 3.2 | 9.7 | 3.7 | 68 | ? |
| Sweden | 2.5 | 8.8 | 3.1 | 80 | yes |
| UK | 2.5 | 7.9 | 3.7 | 56 | yes |
| EC 15 | 2.6 | 7.6 | 3.4 | 75 | |
| Three best | 1.6 | 6.7 | | | |
| Limit | 3.1 | 8.7 | 3.0 | 60 | |

Sources: European Commission Forecasts, cols 1, 3 & 4; *1996 Annual Economic Report*; OECD *Economic Outlook*, December 1995, col. 2.

amount of government investment expenditure and 'the medium-term economic and budgetary position of the Member State'. [58] The reference value of 60% for the ratio of government debt to GDP can likewise be interpreted with a certain flexibility. Although the Bundestag has claimed the right to determine whether the criteria have been properly fulfilled, it will surely accept the positive stance that Chancellor Kohl will certainly adopt, provided that the position regarding the criteria is defensible. As for the EU Council, its decision that any member state's deficit is excessive can be taken only by QMV, and the confidence with which successive European Councils have reaffirmed the progress towards Stage Three suggests in any case that the final decision when it comes in Spring 1998, will not be a matter of low technocracy but of high politics. Germany may well wish to restrict the initial core to a minimum of five or six member states. But a reasonable interpretation of the Treaty could allow the inclusion of several more. **If enlargement and employment are indeed the top policy priorities of the European Union, the decision to proceed with the Euro should surely embrace as many member states as conceivably possible.**

## The British dilemma

The inevitability of a UK general election in the middle of the tricky set of choices about EMU complicates matters for political parties. Given that the decision will have to be made very soon after the election, the conduct of the campaign will do no good to British democracy if the parties do not take up clear positions on EMU. The replacement of sterling by a single currency will be the single most important issue of the next parliament, and, with the IGC, will tend to dominate it. EMU has profound economic and constitutional implications for the UK and deserves to be treated by both parliament and the media with more seriousness and more urgency. The general public, commerce and industry must be allowed to prepare themselves properly for the currency reform, and need clear leadership to do so. Dissembling and prevarication about EMU would surely result in cynicism and disillusion.

In our view, therefore, **the case for the UK now to declare that it will use its best endeavours to participate in Stage Three is strong. This it should do on the basis of a White Paper.** Given the economic threshold required, the political opt-out serves little useful purpose and merely heightens uncertainty. That the UK may well comply with all the convergence criteria in 1997-98 except that of ERM membership makes the decision far from academic, although the ultimate decision about whether to proceed or not will reside with the House of Commons followed, possibly, by a referendum.

Moreover, on the assumption that there will be no delay to the beginning of Stage Three, preparations must begin shortly in the UK to prepare the Bank of England for operational independence of the Treasury. National legislation will have to conform to EU norms for all those member states that are intending at whatever stage to make the transition to Stage Three (Articles 107 and 108). Unless the UK opts out entirely into a third tier of definitive 'outs', the Bank of England will have to be made independent if it is ever to participate in the European System of Central Banks. Primary legislation is needed to give effect to this change. Even if the UK stays out in 1999, Eddie George, Governor of the Bank of England, wants the Bank to be given by Parliament 'a statutory duty to deliver stability'. [60]

It is undeniable that the British opt-out from the ultimate decision about making the transition to Stage Three reduces its influence in all aspects of EMU. Further procrastination will further damage British interests, as the UK's influence over the transitional arrangements (including the pooling of reserves), and in the preparatory discussions about the Stability Pact (including the settlement of fines on errant member states), and in appointments at the European Central Bank, and even, alas, in the choice of name for the currency, is already reduced.

Were such a semi-detached attitude to continue while Britain's partners at the IGC negotiated stability and solidarity arrangements between them, British interests would be badly damaged. There is always the further danger that indifference to British views about EMU could well be succeeded by discrimination against the UK — threatening the integrity of the single market, fuelling more speculation about the future of sterling and forcing a hiking of interest rates. The City of London would probably be the first to suffer, vulnerable as it is to being weakened in the Euro, foreign exchange, banking, bond, equity and derivatives markets.

The economic case for sterling joining the Euro is strong, but has not been put as forcefully as the case against. [61] For our part,

**we believe that British entry would provide a framework for other policies that are needed to improve the performance of the economy.** In order to create a zone of monetary stability, it is in the British interest that France and Germany proceed as quickly as possible to the single currency even if the UK stays out. British membership could help to reverse the tide of nationalism. No further convergence criteria are needed to ensure that EMU is sustainable. A single currency should make a substantial contribution to growth, competitiveness and employment.

As far as the UK is concerned, Labour's position is crucial. The Shadow Chancellor, Gordon Brown, wants 'real convergence' which, he says, 'does not of course mean that we have to have exactly the same levels of output or productivity. What is important is that their trend must not threaten to diverge faster than other means of adjustment in unit costs can cope [with], thereby locking in uncompetitiveness and unemployment'. [62] He proposes the creation of a contra-cyclical European Recovery Fund to invest in employment schemes in a recession and able to run in surplus in a boom.

Europe's business leaders, now including the CBI, are overwhelmingly enthusiastic about the single market, but many of them feel they cannot afford to invest in EMU until member state governments have the political will to implement it. [63] We share that view, and urge that member state governments at the IGC and beyond it use their best endeavours to secure the single currency. There will be short-term dislocation, but the long-term prospects of all Europe will be improved.

With the single currency, a completed single market, a streamlined social model, and tax reform plus a programme for employment, the European Union will have put in place structures that will provide a stimulus to investment and the context for a dynamic economy in the next century. In short, Europe will have found its agenda for prosperity.

# NOTES

[1]  *Federal Trust Papers No. 2, Towards the Single Currency*, London, Federal Trust, May 1995.

[2]  The Presidency Conclusions of the European Council, Madrid, 15-16 December 1995, EC *Bulletin*, 12/95.

[3]  EC Commission White Paper, *Growth, Competitiveness, Employment: The challenges and ways forward into the 21st century*, EC *Bulletin*, Supplement 6/93.

[4]  J.E. Meade, *Full Employment Regained? An Agathotopian Dream*, University of Cambridge Department of Applied Economics Occasional paper 61, Cambridge, CUP, 1995. James Meade (1907-95) was a founder-Patron of the Federal Trust.

[5]  See Centre for Economic Policy Research, Monitoring European Integration 5, *Unemployment: Choices for Europe*, London, CEPR, 1995.

[6]  European Federation for Retirement Provision, Brussels Conference, 18 June 1996.

[7]  Speech to the G7 conference on employment, Lille, 1 April 1996. See also Chirac's article in *Libération*, 25 March 1996.

[8]  See Competitiveness Advisory Group, *Enhancing European Competitiveness*, Second (Ciampi) Report to the President of the European Commission, the Prime Ministers and Heads of State, Luxembourg, December 1995.

[9]  See the formal letter from the European Round Table of Industrialists to Mr Silvio Fagiolo, 15 January 1996.

[10]  For a full discussion of this point see Federal Trust Papers No. 6, *Justice and Fair Play*, London, Federal Trust, April 1996, pp. 33-39.

[11]  See Santer's speech to the European Parliament on 31 January 1996, EC *Bulletin,* 1-2/96.

[12]  Commission Opinion on the IGC 1996, *Reinforcing political union and preparing for enlargement*, Brussels, 1996, para. 13.

[13]  Turin European Council, Presidency Conclusions, 29 March 1996.

[14]  The Pact was approved by the Commission on 5 June following a Round Table with the social partners on 28-29 April 1996. It was discussed at a tripartite conference convened by the Italian presidency on 14-15 June.

[15]  Employment Pact, para. 0.5.

[16]  Employment Pact, para. 5.5.

[17]  See the Editorial by former Commissioner Henning Christophersen in *Challenge 96*, Brussels, Belmont European Policy Centre, Issue 8, May/June 1996.

[18]  Article 103.1.

[19]  See European Commission White Paper, *European Social Policy: A Way Forward for the Union*, COM(94) 333, July 1994; see also TUC General Council, *The European Union: trade union goals*, London, Trades Union Congress, July 1996.

[20]  Jim Northcott, *The Future of Britain and Europe*, London, Policy Studies Institute, 1995, p. 145.

[21]   European Commission, *Eurobarometer*, No. 44, Brussels, Spring 1996, p. 68.

[22]   *Position of the Italian Government on the Intergovernmental Conference for the Revision of the Treaties*, Rome, 18 March 1996, para. III, 1(e).

[23]   See, for example, Report of Council for the Protection of Rural England/ Green Alliance Practitioners' Seminar, *Greening the Treaty*, London, CPRE, May 1995.

[24]   Commission Opinion, op. cit., para. 14.

[25]   *Eurobarometer*, op. cit., p. 68.

[26]   For a fuller discussion of these issues, see Federal Trust Report, *Network Europe and the Information Society*, London, Federal Trust, 1995.

[27]   *Local development and employment initiatives*, COM(95) 273.

[28]   See European Round Table of Industrialists, *Beating the Crisis: A Charter for Europe's Industrial Future*, Brussels, ERT, 1993.

[29]   Declaration No. 18 of the Treaty on European Union.

[30]   The European Investment Fund was set up by the Edinburgh European Council in December 1992, and its capital of Ecu 2 bn is guaranteed jointly by the European Investment Bank, the EU and the commercial sector.

[31]   This was the thrust of the Molitor Report to the European Commission on *Legislative and Administrative Simplification*, presented to the Cannes European Council in June 1995, COM(95) 288. See also the *Reflection Group's Report*, Brussels, December 1995, para. 10.

[32]   Notably Federal Trust Papers No. 3, *Building the Union: reform of the institutions*, London, Federal Trust, June 1995, pp. 22-25.

[33]   For example, Economic and Social Committee, *The EU Internal Market Forum*, Brussels, 1995.

[34]   Commissioner Mario Monti presented a memorandum to this effect to ECOFIN; reprinted in *Agence Europe*, 3 April 1996.

[35]   See *A people's Europe*, London, the Labour Party, 1995; and *Meeting the European Challenge: Proposals for the 1996 Intergovernmental Conference*, London, Liberal Democrats, 1996.

[36]   Commission Opinion, op. cit., para. 12.

[37]   In a speech to the Institute of Directors, January 1996.

[38]   *Agence Europe*, 1-2 April 1996.

[39]   We discuss this issue in Federal Trust Papers No. 5, *Enlarging the Union*, London, Federal Trust, February 1996.

[40]   See Michael Franklin and Jonathan Ockenden, *European Agricultural Policy: Ten Steps in the Right Direction*, Briefing Paper No. 14, London, Royal Institute of International Affairs, November 1994.

[41]   See also the statement on Article 39 by the WWF, Brussels, January 1996.

[42]   For example, the *Economist* argues that, though popular, the European Regional Development Fund is in practice manipulated by member state treasuries to substitute for national public expenditure; the European Social Fund — with Ecu 47 bn to spend between 1994-99 — has had very little practical effect on training people who would not otherwise be trained into long-term new jobs; and the Cohesion Fund is little more than pork-barrel politics, acting as a sweetener to governments who need to carry out unpalatable structural reform of their economies; *The Economist*, 27 January 1996.

[43] The EIB also lent a further Ecu 2.8 bn outside the EU, mostly to Palestine and South Africa.

[44] The UK rebate has been calculated since 1986 as a reduction of its VAT base by two-thirds of the difference between its VAT share and its receipts from the EU budget; Germany's contribution is also reduced by one-third of its normal VAT share.

[45] EC Commission, *Report of the Study Group on the Role of Public Finance in European Integration,* (2 vols), (MacDougall Report), Brussels, 1977.

[46] For a concise discussion of the theory involved, see Dieter Biehl, 'The Public Finances of the Union', Chapter 9 of Andrew Duff, Roy Pryce and John Pinder (eds), *Maastricht and Beyond: Building the European Union*, London, Routledge, 1994. In 1994 the UK made a net contribution to the EU budget of £897 m.

[47] See also Michael Franklin, *The EC Budget: Realism, Redistribution and Radical Reform,* London, Royal Institute of International Affairs, Discussion Papers No. 42, October 1992.

[48] See Federal Trust Papers No. 3, *Building the Union: reform of the institutions*, London, Federal Trust, July 1995, p. 24.

[49] The Federal Trust is grateful for evidence received from Mr N P Hepworth, Director of the Chartered Institute of Public Finance and Accountancy (CIPFA).

[50] See for example Michael Emerson et al., *One Market, One Money*, Oxford, OUP, 1992.

[51] *New Labour, New Life for Britain*, London, Labour Party, July 1996; *A people's Europe*, op. cit.

[52] Speech by Minister Quinn to the TEPSA Conference on the Irish Presidency, Dublin, 24-25 May 1996.

[53] For a discussion on options for a new ERM, see Christopher Taylor, *Exchange Rate Arrangements for a Multi-Speed Europe*, EUI Working Papers, Robert Schuman Centre, Florence, EUI, December 1995.

[54] Article 109j.1.

[55] See European Monetary Institute, *Annual Report 1995*, Frankfurt, April 1996.

[56] Communication from the Commission to the European Council, *Preparation of EMU: Current State of Play*, 12 June 1996.

[57] See the comparable table for 1996 in *Towards the Single Currency*, op. cit., p. 11.

[58] Article 104.c.3.

[59] The Federal Trust is grateful for these figures to Christopher Johnson, author of *In With the Euro, Out With the Pound: the Single Currency for Britain*, London, Penguin, 1996.

[60] House of Lords, 11th Report of the Select Committee on the European Communities, *An EMU of 'Ins' and 'Outs'*, Vol. I, HL Paper 86, June 1996, para. 101.

[61] One of the few exceptions is Quentin Davies MP, *The United Kingdom and Europe: a Conservative view*, The Macleod Essays, No. 4, London, 1996.

[62] Rt Hon. Gordon Brown MP, Speech to the Friedrich Ebert Stiftung, Bonn, 7 May 1996.

[63] See *Building a Europe that works: an Agenda for the IGC*, London, CBI, June 1996; and A survey of executive opinion across Europe, *Economic and Monetary Union: the Business View*, London, Andersen Consulting, January 1996.